TIMOTHY REIGLE

LIVING PORN FREE

10 STEPS TO RECOVERY, REDEMPTION, AND RENEWAL

*To my incredible wife, Ashley, who
stayed with me through the darkest
days of my addiction, always believed
in me, and never gave up.
My recovery and this book are
dedicated to you.*

FOREWORD

Having worked as a counselor in the sex and pornography addiction field for nearly a decade, I have seen recovery materials that are confusing and frustrating to those struggling with these addictions. Instead of offering practical insights and lifestyle changes that can be implemented, those addicted are bombarded with tasks, tasks, and more tasks. For some, recovery work amounts to 20-plus hours a week.

In this day and age, with most of us being pulled in hundreds of directions, individuals do not have a disposal 20-plus hours to put to recovery. Please note, I am not saying recovery should not be a priority, it should. But when it becomes a burden, which many programs make it, we are setting up individuals for failure.

More shame. More discouragement. More failures.

Being encouraged to "try harder" or add more tasks to recovery is not the road to success. Those struggling with sex or porn addictions need to be uplifted and to understand the goal is not merely to remove these destructive sexual behaviors from their lives, but to transform their hearts. We, as mental health professionals, are doing a great disservice to those who need our help if we do not provide a clear path to freedom. That is not the case with Living Porn Free.

In the book you are about to read, you will find a straight-forward and easy-to-implement roadmap for recovery. Timothy lays the groundwork for success clearly and simply so you will not only be able to comprehend the issues he is discussing but will be able to implement them into your life. He understands the importance of helping you to understand what is at the core of your addiction and provides the steps necessary to get you to where you need to be.

Having been trained to integrate theology and psychology in my counseling practice, I appreciate and understand the importance of bringing God and the Holy Spirit into the recovery process. I realize without the strength and reassurance of Jesus Christ, I would not have been able to maintain sobriety that has lasted 20 years. And that is another reason why I admire the work Timothy has done with his book. He demonstrates an excellent example of an integrated approach to recovery utilizing Christian teachings to support clinical practices and tools.

No one, and I mean no one, can navigate the road to recovery if you cannot read the roadmap. But more importantly, you also need to understand the importance of adapting the lifestyle changes that Timothy outlines. His clear-cut direction will enable you to not only get on the right path of recovery, but to maintain long-lasting freedom.

Blessings on your journey.

Eddie Capparucci
LPC, C-CSAS, CPCS
Author of Going Deeper: How the Inner Child Impacts Your Sexual Addiction

TABLE OF CONTENTS

TIMOTHY REIGLE

INTRODUCTION

There is a reason you are reading this book.

This is not a book anyone wandering through a bookstore will pick up and peruse through. You had to seek out this book. Or maybe, it sought out you. Maybe someone bought you this book. Maybe coming across this book was a sign that you finally needed to make a change in your life.

Let's be real. The reason you are reading this book is because you are addicted to pornography. Watching porn and masturbating have become such a part of your life that it has taken control of you. There is nothing you desire to do more. You would rather spend time online watching other people have sex than actually having sex with your spouse. You would rather jerk off than get dressed and go out and spend time with your friends. You would rather spend hours on Pornhub than spend ten minutes doing any sort of physical exercise. You promise yourself the last time was the last time. You get rid of your stash. Then before you know it, you are right back at it again.

Sex has become all you think about. You spend countless hours behind a computer monitor or with a phone in your hand. It has gotten so bad, you can no longer get an erection on command when you go to make love to your wife! Worse yet, she found your internet browser history and now your marriage is on the rocks. You are scared to death the truth of your life will be exposed to the world.

I get it. I've been there. I have battled pornography addiction almost my entire teenage and adult life. And it did not stop there, it spiraled into a total sex addiction. There are sins I am so ashamed to admit that I hate even thinking about it. I disregarded time with my children to pursue my own selfish desires. I chose sex and porn over my family. I lived a secret life. I got caught a bunch of times, but it did not matter. I just got better at lying and better at not getting caught.

I tried for years to stop, to gain control, to turn my life around. I knew what I was doing was self-destructive behavior, but I could not stop. I wanted freedom. I sought counseling. I prayed harder. I tried harder. Nothing worked. The hole just got deeper and deeper and deeper. I was stuck in an endless cycle of addiction.

But then I finally got to the point where enough was enough. I had to look myself in the mirror and confess who I truly was. I hated what I saw. I decided that I finally needed to fight back. It was not a Hollywood style "I've seen the light" moment or anything like that. I did not instantly give up porn or immediately stop having sex with random women. My marriage did not just heal itself and I did not suddenly become an amazing man of God. But it was the start of God making a change in my heart. I finally stopped searching for my fulfillment and purpose in the physical pleasures of this world and looked to God to lead my life. I found when I turned away from the things I used to mask my pain and sought God instead, I found the peace I was looking for. When I opened up about who I truly was on the inside, God opened up pathways for healing. When I confessed my sins to my family, they forgave me.

My prayer is that you have reached the same point in your own life and that is why you are reading this book. I pray you have finally gotten to where you can no longer continue doing the same things over and over again and expect a different result. My prayer is that you now hate your sin more than you love the immediate satisfaction it gives you.

If not, do not waste your own time or my time and just put this book down now.

But if you are ready to finally break free from this addiction, if you are ready to put in the hard work that's required to conquer it, and if you are ready to step up and be the man you can and should be, I welcome you to this journey.

Before we get started, however, I want to be honest with you about a few things.

This book alone will not cure your addiction to pornography. You will not read this book and miraculously not have the urge to look at porn anymore. This book simply gives you a plan and the tools to begin that process.

Breaking free from addiction takes time. It can take years. It involves much more than just reading a book. You need to apply the suggestions I make in this book and live them out for many days, weeks, months, and possibly even years before you see any real progress. There will be setbacks. You will NOT quit porn cold turkey. Do not think you are going to macho man this thing and just stop. You will not. You physically cannot do it. Trust me, I tried.

Lastly, you will only get out of this book what you put into it. Take your time. Do not rush through it. Re-read each chapter if necessary, focusing on each step and how to implement it into your life. Take the time to answer the questions and complete the exercises. If you only skim through it quickly, you will not get very far. But if you take action on the suggestions I offer and do the work that needs to be done, you can find freedom.

You can do it. It will be the hardest thing you have ever done in your life. But by the grace and forgiveness of God, and with the tools I will teach you in this book, you can LIVE PORN FREE.

TIMOTHY REIGLE

1
ADMIT THERE IS A PROBLEM

It may sound cliché, but admitting you have a problem with porn is the first step towards healing. You must admit to yourself that your behavior is destructive, wrong, and unhealthy.

Stop and ask yourself, "Am I actually addicted to porn?"

Answer these questions:

 × Do I feel shameful after watching porn?

 × Does it overwhelm my time?

 × Would I rather watch porn and masturbate than do anything else?

 × Have I had negative consequences as a result of consuming porn yet continued to do it anyway?

 × Does it interfere with my relationship with my wife?

 × Have I tried to quit and failed time and time again?

If you answered yes to any of these questions, there is a good chance you are addicted to porn. It is a sad fact, but the majority of men are.

Research by Covenant Eyes shows:[1]

×   79% of 18-30 year olds; 67% of 31-49 year olds; 49% of 50-68 year olds view pornography at least several times a month

×   63% of 18-30 year olds; 38% of 31-49 year olds; 25% of 50-68 year olds view pornography at least several times a week

×   55% of married men say they watch porn at least once a month, compared to 70% of unmarried men.

It is no better among churched men with studies showing 68% of Christian men regularly view porn, including 50% of pastors.

If you think you might be addicted to porn, you probably are.

There is a test called the Sexual Addiction Screening Test that can help you determine if you have a problem with sexual addiction. Any score at 7 or above indicates problems with sexual behavior.

You can take the test at this website. https://psychology-tools.com/test/sast

Surprised? I know I was. For transparency, my score at the height of my sexual addiction was 37.

Porn is an epidemic. It is a silent cancer wreaking havoc on men and destroying lives and marriages. I have seen what damage porn can do. It nearly destroyed my marriage. It almost broke up my family.

It leads to emotional and psychological problems that the medical community is only beginning to understand. It is causing erectile dysfunction in teenagers! Its effect on the brain is similar

---

[1] "The Most Up-to-Date Pornography Statistics." Covenant Eyes, 2018, www.covenanteyes.com/pornstats/.

to that of hardcore drug users and has been shown to be equally as addictive.

It is all based on a lie! Porn makes you believe that YOU are having sex with that hot model. Porn will never reject you. It does not care if you have put on a few pounds or are so socially awkward that you cannot even talk to a real woman. It drives you further into isolation and further from reality.

In many men, porn addiction, or any addiction, is covering up an issue that we are unable to cope with. Addiction becomes self-medication for a deeper emotional wound. We do not become addicted to the porn, we become addicted to the dopamine release it provides. We are forced to continue seeking more and more to get the same dopamine hit. Porn is just the drug of choice.

But the truth is porn is sin. It corrupts your mind, literally. It is a gateway drug to other sinful behavior. It is pure lust. The Bible tells us to FLEE from sexual immorality. Not just turn it off. Not just turn a blind eye but flee from it. Run away!

Through shame and guilt, this silent cancer has caused wreckage upon too many men's lives.

If you are like I was, your porn addiction has become more than you can control. It may be overwhelming your life and affecting your marriage, your job, and even your overall health.

But there is hope. You can overcome this addiction. The first step to healing is admitting that it is a problem in your life and that you need help. By reading this book, you have already started the process. You are fighting back.

But you need to be honest about your situation. Too often, we lie about our behavior. We lie to our wives, our friends, and especially ourselves. You must be honest with yourself if you have any chance of overcoming this addiction.

You need to admit what you have done. Use the admission exercise at the end of this chapter to make a full disclosure of your actions and behaviors. This will allow you to take full account of what you are struggling with so you can create a plan to fight back.

QUESTIONS TO CONSIDER

**1. Did you answer yes to any of the questions about being addicted to porn?
If so, do you think you are addicted?**

_____

_____

_____

_____

2. Why do you think so many men of all ages are addicted to porn?

_____

_____

_____

_____

**3. What was your score on the Sexual Addiction Screening Test? Did this surprise you?
Did it reveal anything about yourself and your addiction?**

_____

_____

_____

_____

TIMOTHY REIGLE

4. What lies has porn told you?

_____

_____

_____

_____

5. What do you need to be honest about with yourself?

_____

_____

_____

_____

ADMISSION EXCERCISE

The first step to living porn free is to admit you have a problem. Use the exercise below to make a full disclosure of all the negative and addictive behaviors you took part in. Confessing your actions starts the process toward healing. This may take some time. Try to think of everything you have done. You might discover some things you had blocked from your memory. This exercise will allow you to take account of what you are struggling with so you can create a plan to fight back.

It is very important to be 100% honest in this exercise. Too often, men lie about their behavior; both to others and to themselves. If you are going to live porn free, you must be honest with yourself and admit you have a problem.

NOTE: DO NOT immediately share this with your spouse. Disclosure with your wife should take place in a safe and healthy environment under the direction of professional counselor, pastor, or coach.

1. THOUGHTS AND FANTASIES:
My Actions: (Ex. Objectifying women, Fantasies about sex, Flirting)

_____

_____

_____

How Often: (Ex. Daily, 4-5 a week, monthly)

_____

2. PORN
My Actions: (Ex. Hardcore Sex, Oral Sex, Group Sex, Homosexual, Lesbian, Threesomes, Blondes, Teens)

_____

_____

_____

How Often: (Ex. Weekly, Monthly, Occasionally)

_____

3. ACTING OUT:
My Actions: (Ex., Intercourse, Masturbation, Oral Sex, Emotional Affairs, Escorts)

_____

_____

_____

How Often: (Ex. Weekly, Monthly, Occasionally)

_____

4. OTHER COMPULSIONS:
My Actions: (Ex. Drugs, Alcohol, Food, Self-Harm, Smoking)

_____

_____

_____

How Often: (Ex. 10 years, Daily, $100 a month)

_____

5. THE FINANCIAL COST:
My Actions: (Ex. Affairs-Meals, Hotels, etc.; Alcohol and Drugs; Porn-subscriptions/DVDs; Clubs, Prostitutes)

_____

_____

_____

How Often: (Ex. $30,000 / $5,000 / $2,500)

_____

TIMOTHY REIGLE

2
SEEK GOD'S HELP

Pornography addiction is not just a physical problem, a medical problem, or an emotional problem. It is a spiritual problem. True healing only comes through God. Deep down in our hearts we are searching for joy, fulfillment, and purpose.

Porn addiction tries to satisfy those legitimate desires in an illegitimate way.

Michael John Cusick, in his excellent book on sexual addiction, *Surfing For God*, writes:

> *"The man who surfs the web for porn is surfing for God."* [2]

What you are actually seeking out when you look at porn or engage in immoral sexual behavior is the lasting joy, fulfillment, and purpose that only God can provide. You are trying to find your own path to what only He can give you.

I would never have overcome my sexual addiction without my faith in God. He gives us the courage to fight the battle. He gives us the grace and forgiveness we need to heal. And only God can give us the strength to overcome our addiction.

King David, in 2 Samuel chapter 11, committed terrible acts of sexual sin. He committed adultery with a married woman, Bathsheba. When she consequently became pregnant, he tried to entice her husband to come home to cover it up. When that scheme failed, he murdered her husband so he could have her.

---

[2] Cusick, Michael John, Surfing For God (Nashville, Tenn.: Thomas Nelson, 2012), p.15

The prophet, Nathan, confronted David about his actions. David confessed his sin and sought redemption. Psalm 51 is David's cry for forgiveness and redemption from God. I encourage you to read it.

> *"Have mercy on me, O God,*
> *because of your unfailing love.*
> *Because of your great compassion,*
> *blot out the stain of my sins*
> *Wash me clean from my guilt.*
> *Purify me from my sin.*
> *For I recognize my rebellion;*
> *it haunts me day and night.*
> *Against you, and you alone, have I sinned;*
> *I have done what is evil in your sight."*
> *"Purify me from my sins, and I will be clean;*
> *wash me, and I will be whiter than snow."*

David poured out his heart to God. He realized that only in God could he find forgiveness. He asked God to cleanse him from his sin and wash him white as snow.

That is what we seek to do. We realize we are living in sin. We ask for God's forgiveness. We desire to be free from the bondage of sexual sin. We want to be made clean; to live a pure life free from pornography and addiction.

Seeking God's help through prayer and meditation will be your biggest tool in overcoming pornography addiction. God can protect us from the attacks of the enemy who is trying to keep us in bondage.

> *"If God is for us, who can be against us?" Romans 8:31*

You will never win the battle against pornography and sexual addiction on your own. You are not strong enough.

Our human desire is to sin. Our human nature is to seek out the easy path; to look for instant gratification. Our willpower is not strong enough to defeat this addiction.

I am sure you have already tried to quit porn. I am sure you failed at it or you would not be reading this book. Defeating pornography addiction is not a matter of trying harder. Trust me, I tried and tried for years. It did not work.

Discipline is not enough.

I will say that again. Discipline is not enough.

If it were, we would have no problem overcoming addictions. You could just discipline yourself not to look at porn like you discipline yourself to go to the gym.

Doesn't work does it?

Porn addiction is a cycle. You go through a cycle of triggers, rituals, acting out, and shame. You do this over and over again. You feel terrible about your sin and promise yourself that you will never do it again. You may even destroy all the porn in your possession. Then before you know it, you are right back at it again.

We need something to break the cycle. Discipline will not break the cycle because it does not deal with the real problem. Discipline does not address the root issue deep inside of us that we are self-medicating through porn and sex.

Only through the process of God healing your heart, can you break the cycle and overcome addiction to porn.

If you truly want to live a porn free life, get on your knees before God. Go to him in humbleness and prayer, as David did, and ask him to help you fight this battle.

He will give you the strength to overcome.

He will give you the desires of your heart.

He will give you the healing that is necessary to win.

To live porn free, you need God's help.

QUESTIONS TO CONSIDER

1. What are your thoughts on Michael John Cusick's quote, *"The man who surfs the web for porn is surfing for God."*?

_____

_____

_____

_____

2. Can you identify with David in the Bible story? Have you tried to cover up your sin? Was there someone who confronted you like Nathan did?

_____

_____

_____

_____

3. How many times have you tried to quit porn and been unable to?

_____

_____

_____

_____

4. Why is discipline not enough to break the cycle of porn addiction?

_____

_____

_____

_____

5. Are you willing to admit you are not strong enough on your own and need God's help?

_____

_____

_____

_____

_____

TIMOTHY REIGLE

BIBLE READING EXERCISE

The second step to Living Porn Free is to Ask God's Help. The best way to find strength and encouragement from God is through His Word, the Bible. Brothers, everything we need to live a Godly life, a masculine life, and a fulfilling life is found in the pages of Scripture. I have found a method of reading, understanding, and applying Scripture that not only helps me read the Bible more, but helps to make sure I am living out the principles it teaches.

1. Re-Read:
Whatever passage of Scripture you are considering, re-read it several times.

Read it slowly, processing each word in your mind. I have often found it helps to re-read the verse(s) out loud. Hearing them audibly helps you to further capture the passage. Re-reading makes sure you are focusing on the passage and not just skimming over it.

2. Re-Write:
Re-Write the passage out by hand.

Writing the verse out by hand forces you to think through what you are writing. It makes you further process each word one by one. Writing by hand also aids in memorization. Whenever I am trying to memorize something, I always write it out by hand. The act of writing cements the passage into your mind.

3. Re-Word:
Re-Word the passage into your own vocabulary.

Even modern translations of the Bible can sometimes be hard to comprehend. Take the passage that you just wrote out by hand, and re-write it using words that you would use. Write down how you would describe the passage if you had to explain it to someone who had never read it before. Re-wording puts the passage into your perspective and thought patterns.

4. Re-Apply:
Re-Apply the Bible passage to your life.

How can you apply what the verses teach to your own life? Where does it fit into what is going on in your daily walk with Christ? It may be a passage you know well, but if you do not apply the Biblical lessons to your life, you are wasting your time. Write out how the verse applies to your life and what you can do to better live out the commands Scripture gives us.

3
FIND YOUR NATHAN

You will not defeat porn addiction on your own.

Let's face it, you have been trying to overcome it on your own for a long time now and have gotten nowhere. You were hoping it would just go away and no one would ever find out about your secret.

Sorry, brother, it does not work like that.

The truth is, there are millions of other men out there fighting the same battle as you. We suffer in silence. We need to band together as brothers in this battle and help each other fight back.

If you want to live a porn free life, you must have a support partner.

You must find your Nathan.

Most people are not familiar with what happened *after* David's adultery. In 2nd Samuel chapter 12, the prophet Nathan came to David and using a story about a poor man's lamb, manages to make the King realize how badly he has messed up. Throughout David's reign, Nathan was there to support him, provide wisdom, and tell him hard truths when he needed to hear them.

You need other men who will come alongside you, support you, encourage you, and keep you accountable.

A close male friend provides three important things.

1. INTIMACY

Men need an intimate friend. We need someone we can confide in with absolute confidentiality and trust. You need someone who knows your deepest secrets. Having a person who knows you in and out, who knows you better than you know yourself, is worth that friend's weight in gold.

We all require a loyal, devoted friend who has our best interests at heart to listen and be there for us in tough times as well as good times.

Intimacy among men is rarely seen in today's society. It is diminished and often ridiculed. Society cannot separate intimacy from sex. So, they assume that two close, intimate males are "gay" or in a "bromance". When in reality, we need to have deep relationships with other men in order to thrive.

We all desire a friend that will be there for us through thick and thin. Someone who can cry with us, laugh with us, mourn with us, and celebrate with us. We crave that unspoken language between two people, the inside jokes, the comradery. We crave intimacy and having a good, close friend provides that to us.

2. ENCOURAGEMENT

Secondly, close friendships provide us encouragement. They push us to be better. They pick us up when we are feeling down.

When you get knocked down, or you fail in your battle with addiction, he'll come over and help you up, tell you to rub the dirt off your pants and get back in the game.

That is what men do. That is what a good friend will do.

A true friend will never leave another man behind. He will carry him on his shoulders if he must, but he is not leaving him behind.

A close intimate friend encourages you, fights alongside you in battle, has your back, and remains loyal until the end.

To fight this battle with porn, you need a brother to fight alongside you and encourage you.

3. ACCOUNTABILITY

Lastly, deep friendship provides accountability.

A good brother can see through the BS you tell yourself and try to tell others. He will not let you falter or head down the wrong path.

We all need someone who will tell us what we need to hear instead of what we want to hear.

Especially when dealing with issues of porn addiction and sexual purity, we need a brother who will check up on us and make sure we are doing what we are supposed to be doing.

We all need a Nathan to keep us accountable for our actions. Rebuking King David like Nathan did was of great risk. The king could have had him killed for speaking so bluntly to him. But that's exactly what David needed. He needed a friend to show him his errors. His ego would not allow him to see it himself.

I would never have recovered from my sinful past if I did not have friends who came and slapped some sense into me. They took me to task for my mistakes and made sure I realized where I had gone wrong.

As men, if we do not have someone looking out for us, our own selfish desires and arrogance can take us down some very dark paths. We need brothers to keep us accountable and hold our feet to the floor.

It is critical to have someone who you can go to for advice and direction. When we do not have all the answers, we should have that person we can rely on to give us an honest opinion. A good brother will tell you what he thinks whether you like it or not.

Who can be this type of friend and support system for you?

First of all, it MUST be a man. Under no circumstances whatsoever should your support partner be a female. First for the obvious reasons. Second, we are dealing with a male issue. You need another man who can understand what you are going through. I do not care if you are very close with a sister, or your mother, or whoever. Your support partner cannot be a female.

Second, it helps greatly if your support partner has battled addiction himself. You need someone who knows what you are going through, who knows the battlefield, and has found a path through the mines. He will warn you of situations to steer clear of and advise you on what methods work to overcome addiction. They know what you are going through because they have been there before.

A friend who is *currently* going through the battle is also helpful. You can work together to support each other and keep each other accountable.

Let's also take a look at what you are NOT looking for.

Your support partner must not be your wife. Your wife should be aware of your addiction and should certainly be a part of your recovery. But she must not be your accountability partner.

In this battle, there will be many ups and downs. You need to discuss those ups and downs with your close friend. You need to tell him every time you are tempted or relapse.

All this will do to your wife is discourage her and reopen the wounds that you already caused.

Second, your support system must not be someone who does not see porn as a problem. If they are going to help you, they need to understand that what you are doing is wrong and you are trying to improve your life.

If they do not understand that, they are not your friend.

Lastly, your support system should not be someone who has been negatively affected by your addiction. I had a close friend who ended up being just as hurt by my sin and addiction as my wife was. In a way, we were *too* close of friends for him to be my accountability partner.

For the same reasons, it also should not be an immediate family member. It should not be your father, or brother, or son, etc. It can be someone related to you, but it should not be someone that is a part of your nuclear family. Your close family members are often victims of your sin as much as your wife is.

Now that you know the type of friend you are looking for, where do you find men like this?

A good place to start is church. A pastor or church leader is a great person to have for your support system.

In fact, I strongly recommend you talk to a pastor. Even if he is not your direct accountability partner, he can still help you through this fight and pray with you.

You may also need to see a counselor. However, I recommend someone who specializes in addictive behavior. Many counselors and even pastors have little or no experience with addiction and do not understand the unique circumstances that come along with pornography and sexual bondage.

Seeing a specialist can help you work through some of the emotional parts of recovery from addiction.

Or just talk to one of your close friends. If he is truly your friend and loves you, he will understand and want to help you.

Another option for a strong support system is coaching. I offer one-on-one coaching if you feel you need someone to come alongside and support you in your battle. I provide personal guidance to create a plan to fight your addiction and accountability to keep you on track. Contact me at timothy@intothewildernessblog.com or Direct Message me on Twitter @TimothyReigle if one-on-one coaching could help in your battle to live porn free.

I know it is hard to open yourself up and expose your deep secrets to another man. But you cannot fight this battle alone. You need help. You need support. You need accountability.

In order to live porn free, you need a strong support system.

QUESTIONS TO CONSIDER

1. Why do you think it is so hard for men to overcome porn addiction alone?

_____

_____

_____

_____

2. Do you understand true intimacy? Do you have intimate relationships in your life that are not sexual?

_____

_____

_____

_____

3. Are there people in your life that are cheerleaders for you? Who can you look to for an encouraging word?

_____

_____

_____

_____

4. Why is accountability so important? What does an accountability partner do for you? Who can be your Nathan?

_____

_____

_____

_____

5. How do you think having a coach as your support system could help you in your battle with porn addiction?

_____

_____

_____

_____

TIMOTHY REIGLE

TELL YOURSELF EXERCISE

Many men's problem with porn started in boyhood. At that young and impressionable age, you learned you could use porn and sex to "escape" from negative emotions and situations. In order to dispel some of the lies you learned to believe at that age, list ten things that you wish you could say to your 6-16-year-old self. What advice would you give? What encouragement would you offer? Are there things you would warn him about?

1. _____

2. _____

3. _____

4. _____

5. _____

6. _____

7. _____

8. _____

9. _____

10. _____

TIMOTHY REIGLE

4
JOIN A MEN'S SUPPORT GROUP

In order to find freedom from pornography and sexual addiction, you need to join a group of men working together to improve their lives.

You need to find a men's sexual purity group.

Support groups go beyond your individual support system to help and encourage you in your battle with addiction.

You need a Nathan, an intimate friend and accountability partner, yes, but you also need a group of men to share with, pray with, and support each other.

There is a reason Alcoholics Anonymous and other support groups have been so popular and successful. They work!

You cannot fight this battle alone. Meeting regularly with a support group provides an opportunity to share your own struggles and learn from others about theirs. You can gain advice from men going through the same battle you are. And eventually, you will be able to guide other men through it too.

Meeting with a men's support group allows for a regular check-in. They help you stay on track and keep your goals fresh in your mind. Acknowledging your problem in a group setting allows others hold you accountable.

They also help you learn. Many sexual purity groups work through a book or curriculum designed to help men overcome sexual addiction. These lessons help you learn about your addiction and why men are so susceptible to porn. They will educate you about how the brain works and what porn addiction does to you physically and medically.

There are many different groups and programs that offer support to men suffering with sexual addiction. If you are not sure where to begin or where to find one, ask your pastor. Many pastors will know of groups meeting locally in your area.

Another way is just to Google it. Just a simple search will bring up many different groups that you can reach out to for help.

Here are a few groups that I am familiar with and recommend.

1. CONQUER SERIES

https://conquerseries.com/

Conquer Series is a DVD series and book program that I have personally completed. I also help lead a group at my local church. The program takes you through 10 DVD lessons offering education, encouragement, and tools to conquer your addiction. You can find where local groups are meeting on their website.

2. EVERY MAN'S BATTLE

https://newlife.com/emb/

Every Man's Battle is a book series written by Stephen Arterburn and Fred Stoeker. They offer several different books and workbooks that are incredibly helpful to men in the battle. Many churches lead small groups through this book.

Every Man's Battle also offers monthly weekend workshops throughout the United States. The workshops are a three-day intense program to help men in "crisis" mode with their addiction. They are almost like an acute weekend rehab for men suffering from sexual addiction. I have personally been to one of these weekends and it was life changing. They mix large group education with small group sharing to build relationships, provide tools to fight back, and give you a plan to help overcome. You can find a workshop close to you on their website.

3. PURE DESIRE

https://puredesire.org

I have personally worked with counselors and Pastors from Pure Desire. They will connect you with both local and online groups to help you or a loved one who is battling pornography addiction

4. SEXAHOLICS ANONYMOUS

https://www.sa.org/

Sexaholics Anonymous is a twelve-step program similar to Alcoholics Anonymous. There are a number of different twelve-step programs specializing in sexual addiction. Sex Addicts Anonymous, Sexual Compulsives Anonymous, and Sexual Recovery Anonymous are a few.

5. FIGHT THE NEW DRUG

https://fightthenewdrug.org/

Fight The New Drug is an online advocacy group spreading awareness about the dangers of pornography and the damage it can cause. They have a number of resources on their website that are very helpful.

6. XXX CHURCH

https://www.xxxchurch.com

XXX Church was founded by a youth pastor and is now run by a former porn star. They provide resources to battle porn addiction and are one of the leading voices against pornography.

7. COVENANT EYES

https://www.covenanteyes.com

Covenant Eyes provides website blocking software you can install on your computer, phone and other devices which block access to porn sites. They also offer many great resources for fighting porn addiction.

In addition to these resources, there are thousands of local organizations and churches that have set up sexual addiction support groups.

Talk to your pastor or counselor or even your doctor. They should have information on local organizations that can help you in your battle.

I know it is not easy and can be awkward to join one of these groups. But the lessons you can learn, the tools you will receive, and the friendship and support you will gain is vital to winning your battle.

Finding and attending a support group is essential to living porn free.

QUESTIONS TO CONSIDER

1. Why is working together with a group of men important in overcoming porn addiction?

_____

_____

_____

_____

_____

2. What does a regular meeting with other men fighting the battle provide?

_____

_____

_____

_____

_____

3. Have you looked into a men's support group in your area?

_____

_____

_____

4. Would having blocking software on your devices help you to avoid porn?

_____

_____

_____

_____

5. Where can you go to in order to find information on support groups?

_____

_____

_____

_____

VISUALIZATION EXERCISE

1. Write out a word picture of what your life would be like in five years if you continue in your addiction. What would your marriage or relationship be like if you do not solve this problem? Where would you be at emotionally, spiritually, and physically? What negative things would happen if you continued down the path you are on?

_____

_____

_____

_____

2. Write out a word picture of what your life will be like in five years when you defeat your addiction. What will your marriage be like? Where will you be at spiritually and emotionally? How much better off will you be financially? What good things will happen when you decide to take the steps needed to overcome your addiction?

_____

_____

_____

_____

TIMOTHY REIGLE

5
DISCOVER WHY YOU ARE ADDICTED

This will by far be the hardest step to living porn free.

In order to overcome your addiction, you need to understand what is causing it in the first place.

For most men, pornography addiction actually has nothing to do with sex. You do not just have a higher sex drive. It is not that you are just horny all the time. It is not that you are getting something sexual out of it that you are not receiving from your wife.

Porn addiction may have started from a place of sexual curiosity or the need for sexual release, but eventually it became a way to self-medicate some type of pain in your life. There is an underlying wound that you are using porn to cope with.

At orgasm, your brain releases a hormone called dopamine. Dopamine is a neurotransmitter your body produces in the hypothalamus that sends messages from one brain cell to another. Dopamine is the neurotransmitter that controls how you feel pleasure. If you do something pleasurable, dopamine is released. It is your built-in reward system. When you experience something you like, your brain releases dopamine.

When you repeat a particular behavior that releases dopamine, your brain actually creates new "neural pathways" to get you there faster. It creates a shortcut. Eventually you need more and more dopamine to receive the same feeling of pleasure.

This is what causes the addiction. Your brain has literally rewired itself to demand whatever stimulus gives you that dopamine release. With us, it is porn. Porn gives you a HUGE rush of dopamine and a host of other hormones. It makes you feel good, so you want to do it over and over again.

You have become addicted to the dopamine release, not the porn itself. It makes you go back to it again and again for another "hit". When you feel a certain way, you go to porn to make yourself feel better. As your addiction worsens, you need more and different stimuli to give you a larger dose of dopamine.

The difference between porn addiction and other chemical addictions is this. With addictions such as alcohol and hard drugs, you simply crave more. But with porn addiction, you crave different. An alcoholic just pounds more and more vodka. But a porn addict does not watch the same video over and over again. Instead, he is constantly looking for something different; something new and novel. Because of this, porn addiction often escalates into more hardcore and fetish style porn and eventually into webcams, hookups, prostitutes, etc.

For many men, this process of dopamine addiction was learned at a young age. You may have discovered that anytime you faced something negative in life, you could go to porn and get a big dump of dopamine to make yourself feel better or to "escape".

It then became self-medication. Instead of dealing with whatever is making you feel bad, you go to porn to give you a shortcut to feeling better through the dopamine release. But then you feel shameful for your actions, because deep down you know it is wrong. So, you get angry with yourself or you feel depressed. Then after a while, something triggers you and you start the cycle back to the porn again. Round and round you go.

This is why defeating addiction is so difficult. It is not merely breaking bad habits. It is learning how to properly cope with and process emotional pain.

Dealing with that pain is what it takes to overcome porn and sex addiction. Anything else is only treating the symptoms.

You can have all the software blockers in the world, you can attempt to avoid triggers, you can read every book on porn addiction there is, none of it will provide lasting healing until you deal with the emotional pain in your life. You have to stop running away from pain and turn around and face it.

TIMOTHY REIGLE

Dr. Ted Roberts writes:

> *"Sexual bondage is not about sex. It's about how you've learned to medicate the pain in your life. Once you start facing this, your pain level will actually go up. Because you've been medicating that pain for so long, you'll have to put your big boy pants on, and you'll have to face the pain."* [3]

It is a double-edged sword. You need to face the pain in order to heal, but addressing it actually causes more pain. This is why relapse is so common among recovering porn and sex addicts.

Once you start peeling off those layers of Band-Aids and expose the wound, it hurts all over again and you want to run right back to your addiction for relief.

This moment is where sexual addiction is defeated.

You must learn to sit with those emotions and feel them, process them, and manage them in a healthy way. You need to grieve the pain of any loss you have experienced. You need to forgive the wrongs that were done to you. You need to dispel the painful lies about yourself you have come to believe. This process is what breaks you free from the bonds that hold you captive to your addiction.

Often help is needed to do this. This addiction cannot be defeated alone. Coaching and counseling can help you work through the pain and learn to process it.

You need to discover why you are addicted. You need to discover the wound that is causing the pain you are using porn and sex to cope with.

Maybe it was abuse you suffered as a child. Maybe it is an ever-present fear of failure or rejection. It could be depression. It could be a feeling of inadequacy. Maybe it is shame from a sinful past that you would rather hide from. Maybe it was your parent's divorce or a bad breakup. It could be a number of different things.

---

[3] Conquer Series - The Battle Plan For Purity (Stuart, FL : Kingdom Works Studios, 2017) p. 33

Use the "What Are My Wounds" exercise at the end of this chapter to help discover what some of your emotional wounds might be.

In order to find freedom, you must identify that inner emotional wound. It can be difficult to discover what that deeply seated pain is.

To identify your wound, you need to break apart your addictive cycle and retrace the steps you took to seeking out porn.

In the military, whenever there is an engagement, the officers involved must file an After-Action Report. This is an explanation for what happened, what led up to it, and what their response was. The term they often use for the start of an event is called "bang". Anything leading up to that event, is referred to as being "left of bang".

On a timeline, "bang" is on the far right. The event immediately preceding the bang is just to the left. The event preceding that is just a little farther to the left. It keeps going farther and farther left until you get to the original cause.

This type of "After Action Report" is what you must do to identify what led you to seek out porn.

After you have looked at porn and/or masturbated, you are probably feeling pretty terrible. There is a feeling of shame and regret. But you need to take the time to retrace your steps.

What happened right before you looked at porn? What were you doing? What were you feeling? What were the circumstances that led to acting out? Were you home alone? Were you feeling angry? Depressed? Frustrated?

You need to connect the dots in the cycle of shame. What in that cycle caused you to go down the path that led to acting out and looking at porn? Trace the line back "left of bang" until you are able to figure out what emotions led to it.

This is an extremely difficult and complicated thing to do. It may be beneficial to work with a coach, counselor or professional to help you identify your wounds and triggers.

For me, when I felt angry, I went to porn. When I was depressed, I went to porn. Feelings of anxiety sent me down that path. It all led back to the wound of never feeling good enough. I always felt inadequate. The fear of rejection was always present. Several traumatic events in my teenage years made me feel worthless and I spent years trying to cover up for those feelings with sex and porn.

The feeling of "enough" was always the next girl away. If I hooked up with one more girl, or looked at one more video, it would finally be "enough". But it never was.

Something, a wound, a feeling, a traumatic event started you down that path to porn addiction. It is these core emotional triggers that you are using porn to escape from.

You need to discover it, and face it head on, or you will never find healing.

Michael John Cusick writes in Surfing For God:

> *"Have you ever asked yourself what's really going on beneath your craving for porn? What lies below your desire for a pleasurable, physical release? What is your heart's real desire, the legitimate need desperately crying out to be heard? It's called joy."*

Beneath all the addiction and shame is a legitimate desire. You want to feel joy. You want to feel love. Something in your hearts got messed up and you are looking for that feeling in all the wrong places.

Instead of seeking your joy and purpose in God, you have become addicted to the quick fix of the porn dopamine dump. Instead of finding love and fulfillment from healthy relationships, your wound has damaged your brain and you seek out that feeling from porn. But that feeling is fleeting, and you have to come back searching for it again and again.

---

[4] Cusick, Michael John, Surfing For God (Nashville, Tenn.: Thomas Nelson, 2012),p.24

In order to fight back against the addictive cycle, you have to find the wound and face the pain.

It is going to hurt. It may cause you to relapse when you start discovering the inner pain in your heart. That is normal.

But until you discover what is causing the pain that leads to the addictive behavior, you will never find healing.

Discovering why you are addicted and learning to embrace and process pain in a healthy way is the path to living porn free.

QUESTIONS TO CONSIDER

1. Explain how dopamine causes porn addiction.

_____

_____

_____

_____

2. Are there wounds or trauma in your life that you might be using porn to self-medicate?

_____

_____

_____

_____

3. Use the "Left of Bang" exercise to analyze your last relapse.

_____

_____

_____

_____

4. What patterns have you noticed when you use porn? (time of day, home alone, after watching tv, etc.)

_____

_____

_____

_____

_____

5. What do you feel that you are truly searching for when you seek out porn?

_____

_____

_____

_____

TIMOTHY REIGLE

WHAT ARE MY WOUNDS?

In the following table, list ten moments from your life that hurt emotionally. It could be abuse. It could be a fear of failure or rejection, or a feeling of not being "good enough". Maybe it is a past sin or your parent's divorce, or a bad breakup. It could be a number of different things. This will help you identify wounds that may be leading to your addiction. Then identify what things you might have believed as a consequence of those moments, or vows that you made to yourself as a result of them.

EMOTIONAL WOUNDS	WHAT I BELIEVE/VOWS MADE
Example: I was embarrassed by a girl as a teenager	I mess everything up. I will never open myself up emotionally again
Example: My father used to beat me	I am not good enough. I don't deserve love
1.	
2.	
3.	
4.	

EMOTIONAL WOUNDS	WHAT I BELIEVE/VOWS MADE
5.	
6.	
7.	
8.	
9.	
10.	

TIMOTHY REIGLE

6
REMOVE TRIGGERS

Now that you have been able to identify some of the underlying issues that have caused your porn addiction, you need to remove things from your life that cause you to continue in the addictive cycle.

You need to remove and avoid triggers.

Dr. Robert Weiss, a leading expert on sexual addiction defines a trigger as:

> *"Any internal or external catalyst that creates a desire for you to look at pornography"*

Basically, if something causes you to want to look at porn or masturbate, it is a trigger.

Triggers can be anything. They could be a feeling that you have. They can be something that you see that causes you to start down the path to porn. They can be a scenario you find yourself in which makes it easy for you to slip up.

Triggers can be both external and internal.

External triggers can be:
  × Exposure to sexual images (TV, Movies, Magazines, Social Media)
  × Being alone without something to do
  × Argument with your spouse/girlfriend
  × Bad day at work
  × Financial stress
  × Any type of unexpected event (good or bad)

Internal triggers can be:
- × Anger
- × Depression
- × Boredom
- × Stress
- × Loneliness
- × Anxiety

Triggers lead to Fantasizing (You start thinking and daydreaming about sex or porn)

Fantasizing leads to Ritualization (You go to your favorite website or go lock yourself in your room)

Ritualization then leads to Acting Out (Actually looking at porn and masturbating)

Identifying what your triggers are is essential to breaking your addictive cycle and living porn free.

The "left of bang" exercise from Chapter 5 can help you identify triggers.

After you have looked at porn, retrace your steps to how you got there. What feelings did you have or what events took place that started you down the path towards acting out?

Being alone, work stress, and exposure to sexual images were external triggers that lead me down the path to acting out.

Some of my biggest internal triggers were anxiety, stress, and frustration. I would feel overwhelmed and would go to porn for relief.

Once you identify the triggers that cause you to seek out porn, you need to take steps to remove them from your life or minimize exposure to them.

In his "Sermon on the Mount" in the Gospel of Matthew, Jesus discusses removing things from your life that cause you to sin.

Matthew 5:29-30

> *"So, if your eye—even your good eye—causes you to lust, gouge it out and throw it away. It is better for you to lose one part of your body than for your whole body to be thrown into hell. And if your hand—even your stronger hand—causes you to sin, cut it off and throw it away. It is better for you to lose one part of your body than for your whole body to be thrown into hell."*

There is quite a bit of argument on this particular passage. I do not think that Jesus was necessarily encouraging self-mutilation. I believe he was using an extreme example to prove the point that we need to remove whatever is causing us to sin from our lives. This may sometimes require extreme measures.

If seeing sexual scenes on a T.V. show triggers your brain to want to look at porn, stop watching those shows. You might even have to remove the T.V. from your home.

If you are tempted to look at porn late at night when everyone else is in bed, make sure you go to bed when everyone else does to remove that temptation.

If anxiety or frustration are triggers for you, you need to seek ways to deal with those emotions, so they do not lead you down the path toward porn.

Smartphones are one of the most dangerous things a porn addict can have. Many men who are addicted to porn access it exclusively on a smartphone. You have constant, free access to porn in your pocket anytime, anywhere. You may have to go back to an old-fashioned flip phone if you cannot resist the temptation to look at porn on your phone. Remember, Jesus said if it causes you to sin, get rid of it!

For some people, I know that is not possible with how dependent we are on our phones these days. In this case, there is software that you can install on your phone that blocks pornography and other sexual sites. They can also alert your accountability partner if you try to access porn on your device. The software can be installed on your phone, tablet, computer, etc.

Covenant Eyes, https://www.covenanteyes.com is one of the best software applications available.

Another common trigger is social media. Many men are triggered by images they see on Instagram, Facebook, and Twitter. If social media is a problem for you, delete it. You may think you can avoid looking at the "models" on social media, but why take the risk? Get rid of it!

Whatever your triggers may be, you need to find ways to eliminate them completely from your life. If you cannot eliminate them, you must find a way to minimize your exposure to them. Sometimes this takes drastic measures as Jesus explained in the passage from Matthew 5.

But no matter how hard you try to avoid and remove triggers; you WILL still be exposed to them. There is no way to 100% avoid triggers. The enemy (Satan) will make sure of that.

You will be doing great in your battle and avoiding situations that lead you down the path towards acting out, then all of a sudden BOOM! Some trigger will smack you in the face.

You must learn how to react when faced with a trigger.

Here is a great way to remember what to do when you are faced with a trigger.

Remember the "Four R's".

1. REMOVE YOURSELF OR THE TRIGGER

Get the hell out of there! Remove yourself from the situation. Get as far away from the trigger as you can. Or Remove the trigger. Throw it away or turn it off. The Bible tells us to flee from sexual immorality. So, when faced with something that triggers you, get away from it!

2. RE-ENGAGE YOUR MIND

Instead of letting the trigger get a foothold in your mind, immediately re-engage your mind on something else. Do something that requires focus and concentration. Some great things to do are to read a book, exercise, work on something with your hands, or engage in conversation with someone. That way your mind will not dwell on the trigger and you can focus your thoughts on positive things.

3. REACH OUT TO YOUR SUPPORT SYSTEM

These are the moments that your support and accountability partner is there for. If you are feeling anxious or depressed and starting to return to that cycle, call for help! Talk to someone who can walk you through what you are feeling and support you. They can be there for you and lift you up when you are feeling weak and susceptible.

4. REFLECT THROUGH SCRIPTURE, PRAYER, AND JOURNALING

Every time Jesus was tempted by the devil in the wilderness, He responded by quoting Scripture. When you are triggered, open your Bible, and find strength. Even better, memorize particular verses and repeat them over and over when you are tempted. Pray to God to give you strength and help you to avoid the temptation. Psalm 46:1 says, *"God is our refuge and strength, always ready to help in times of trouble"*. This is also a good time to journal your thoughts and emotions. Use the "Left of Bang" exercise to identify triggering emotions and situations.

Living porn free is a battle. You must identify the tools the enemy uses to try and destroy you. You must then try to avoid or remove those triggers from your life.

And when you are inevitably faced with triggers, you must be able to respond appropriately to avoid going down the same old paths. Removing and responding to triggers will help you to live porn free.

QUESTIONS TO CONSIDER

1. What is the difference between External Triggers and Internal Triggers?

_____

_____

_____

_____

2. Explain the addictive cycle that triggers cause.

_____

_____

_____

_____

3. After reading the passage from Matthew 5, what are some things you may need to remove from your life that are causing you to sin?

_____

_____

_____

_____

TIMOTHY REIGLE

4. What are some common triggers that lead you to look at porn?

_____

_____

_____

_____

5. What are the four responses to use when you are faced with a trigger?

_____

_____

_____

_____

TRIGGERS EXERCISE

Identify Five External Triggers

1. _____

2. _____

3. _____

4. _____

5. _____

Identify Five Internal Triggers

1. _____

2. _____

3. _____

4. _____

5. _____

List Ways You Can Use The "4 Rs" when faced with a trigger.

1. Remove The Trigger
What can you remove from your life that causes you to be triggered?

_____

2. Re-Engage Your Mind
What can you do to re-focus your mind and avoid fantasizing?

_____

3. Reach Out To Your Support System
Who can you reach out to for help?

_____

4. Reflect through Scripture, Prayer, and Journaling
How can reading Scripture, Prayer, and Journaling help you to resist temptation?

_____

TIMOTHY REIGLE

7
JOURNAL YOUR PROGRESS

Keeping a journal or diary was part of almost every man's life for centuries.

Many of the historical accounts we have from major events are taken from journals and diaries of the individuals involved. Their journals give us a glimpse into their mind and allow us to travel back in time.

We have gotten away from this habit in modern society.

Journaling helps to focus your thoughts and process what is going through your mind. The act of writing requires you to think and be able to express what you are feeling.

I recommend taking time each night before you go to bed to write down your thoughts. Make it part of your evening routine. Record whether it was a good day or a tough one. Write out what was going through your mind if you were tempted.

There is no right or wrong way to journal. Some people have a set format that they use to record their thoughts each night. Others just sit down with pen and paper and let it flow. It does not have to be narrative. It can simply be a list of your thoughts.

Keeping a journal of your progress in your battle with porn addiction is an excellent way to stay on track. If you do slip up and look at porn or act out, record what happened in your journal. Write down when, where, and what happened. Jot down all the thoughts that were going through your mind when it occurred. Note any triggers that led you to act out. Examine your emotions and what you might have been feeling before things went bad.

Keep track of how many days you go without a slip up. You can later look through these logs and identify patterns. Maybe you are more susceptible on a particular day of the week versus another. Maybe the days that you do not journal are days that you are weaker.

In addition to journaling your bad days, record your good days as well.

Celebrate victories that you have over addiction. If you were tempted and successfully avoided a relapse, celebrate that! Building on small victories creates momentum in your battle with porn.

You need to shift your mindset from focusing on failures to focusing on victories. Maybe you had a relapse after two weeks. You might think "I just threw away two weeks of progress!" No, you did not. You had two weeks of victories and one momentary slip up. Stop beating yourself up over small setbacks and instead celebrate the victories you have, no matter how small.

Make sure you are consistent with your journaling. You will not receive the full benefits of journaling if you only do it occasionally. I have found the longer I go without journaling the more likely I am to mess up.

Journaling keeps me focused and attentive to triggers and other attacks that will cause me to falter. Journaling keeps my guard up. It keeps my goals and the tools I use to avoid temptation in the forefront of my mind.

It is possible to keep a journal on a computer or device, but I strongly recommend using an old-fashioned handwritten journal. I know you may hate writing by hand. I do too and my hand-writing sucks. But the act of writing your thoughts out by hand forces you to think through what you are writing. It makes you think in linear terms and put your thoughts in proper order.

I would encourage you to combine your journaling with your daily scripture, prayer, and meditation.

We discussed in Chapter 2 the importance of seeking God's help in our battle with addiction. Write out your prayers to God. Write down what you want to pray for. Then go through them one by one as you pray.

TIMOTHY REIGLE

If there is a particular passage of Scripture you are working through, write out the passage or a portion of it by hand. It will help you analyze the verse and consider it more deeply. I often re-write the verse in my own words to gain a better understanding of the message God is trying to give to me.

Keeping a journal is an effective tool to living porn free. Pick up a journal at your local store. Use a notebook or even loose paper.

Take the time to record your thoughts and what is happening in your life. Keep track of your progress in your battle with porn addiction.

QUESTIONS TO CONSIDER

1. Why do you think modern men have stopped journaling?

_____

_____

_____

_____

2. How can you establish the habit of daily journaling in your life?

_____

_____

_____

_____

3. How can journaling help you to analyze your addiction?

_____

_____

_____

_____

TIMOTHY REIGLE

4. Why is journaling with pen and paper better than journaling digitally?

_____

_____

_____

_____

_____

5. Create a plan to begin journaling. If you prefer, create a rubric that you use to record your thoughts each day.

_____

_____

_____

_____

_____

JOURNALING EXCERCISE

Use this guide to help you get started in journaling.
List three "Wins" that you had today: They can be something such as successfully avoiding a trigger, completing your daily Bible reading, or having a good date with your wife. It does not have to be something monumental every day. Sometimes just getting through the day in one piece is a win! Focus on positive things that you can build on.

1. _____

2. _____

3. _____

List three things that you can improve on: Maybe you had a rough day and let temptation get the best of you. Or maybe you got unnecessarily short with your wife. The goal here is not to beat yourself up on mistakes, but to list things that you can work towards to improve your life and set yourself up for more victories.

1. _____

2. _____

3. _____

List three things that you are grateful for: Gratitude is incredibly important in living a happy life. Take the time to record some ways that you are blessed. Maybe you are thankful for a job that is fulfilling. Maybe you are grateful for the friend who is always there to support you. By keeping a gratitude journal, you keep things in perspective and allow yourself to remain positive.

1. _____

2. _____

3. _____

8
FIND HEALTHY WAYS TO RELEASE TENSION

You have been using porn as a release. As we have discussed, you use it to self-medicate deeper emotional issues. You also use it to release stress and anxiety. Now that you are hopefully no longer looking at porn, you need other healthy ways to find release.

Men are designed to be physical. We are designed to be active. One of the best ways to avoid falling back into your old habits is to stay active and fit. If you do not already, start going to a gym or working out at home.

Besides the obvious health benefits, lifting weights provides focus. It provides a feeling of accomplishment. Fitness helps to ward off depression and anxiety. Lifting also gives you a way to release aggression. Men are naturally aggressive. We are inherently violent. There is nothing wrong with that. It is how we were designed.

Men were made to be warriors. We were designed for battle. We need a battle to fight. The world has evolved so that men no longer need to be warriors to simply survive, but we do need a battle to fight. Fitness gives us that physical "battle" that our bodies and our instincts crave.

Make sure you do not ignore your nutrition. If all you are eating is junk food, you are going to feel lousy. Improving your diet will help you feel better, have more energy, and will improve your brain function. All of this will lead you too feeling stronger and give you an advantage in avoiding temptations.

Another great way to release physical tension and stay fit is to venture into the great outdoors. Go for a walk or a hike. Ride your bicycle. Play some type of outdoor sports. Staying inside and avoiding any exercise will only exacerbate your porn problem.

You cannot stay isolated and expect to overcome this addiction. You need to get out and experience life. The sunshine and vitamin D will do wonders for your mood and health which, in turn, will help avoid some of the depression and poor moods that can often lead to a relapse.

Playing sports is a great way to release tension and get exercise. I coach my church softball team in the spring. Not only does this provide me with an opportunity for fitness, it also provides relationships with other men that can help me in my battle with addiction. In Chapter 3, we discussed the importance of a support system of friends. Playing team sports provides a perfect place to find men who can help you.

Personally, I love hiking. It requires no equipment, it is cheap, and all you need is your own two feet. Hiking gets you outdoors into God's beautiful creation. I also recommend doing it without any technology. Go for a hike or walk without your earbuds to listen to music. Do not have any distractions or entertainment. Just get yourself outside and clear your mind.

Seek some adventure in your life. Our lives are way too planned and scheduled. Someday, just go out on an adventure. See where the road takes you.

Men need healthy avenues for adventure. Adventure is built into the male psyche going back to the hunter-gatherer societies of ancient times.

John Eldredge, in his groundbreaking book on Christian masculinity Wild At Heart writes:

> *"Many men fall into an affair not for love, not even for sex, but, by their own admission, for adventure."* [5]

If we do not find adventure in a healthy way, we will seek it out in counterfeit ways like sex addiction, porn, and other risky behaviors.

---

[5] Eldredge, John. Wild At Heart - Discovering The Secret Of A Man's Soul. Thomas Nelson, 2010, p. 45

TIMOTHY REIGLE

Eldredge goes on to write:

> "In the heart of every man is a desperate desire for a battle to fight, an adventure to live, and a beauty to rescue."[6]

We are in a battle. We must find the adventure through fitness and physical release. Lastly, we need the beauty.

That leads us to one of the best ways to release physical tensions when trying to overcome sexual addiction. Have sex!

With your wife, that is.

Nothing bonds a married couple together like sex. Having regular sex with your spouse brings you closer together. It unites you in the intimacy that God intended marriage to be. And it gives you the sexual release that you are no longer getting from porn.

But Timothy, my wife doesn't want to have sex with me!

Well, if she has been hurt by your sinful actions, that is completely understandable, and there may be a time period where she is too hurt to be intimate with you.

You should give her this space.

But a wife should not withhold sex for any significant amount of time as punishment for your sin. This helps no one.

In fact, Scripture says we are NOT to withhold sex from each other.

---

[6] Eldredge, John. Wild At Heart - Discovering The Secret Of A Man's Soul. Thomas Nelson, 2010, p. 9-10

1 CORINTHIANS 7:5

> *"Do not deprive each other of sexual relations, unless you both agree to refrain from sexual intimacy for a limited time so you can give yourselves more completely to prayer. Afterward, you should come together again so that Satan won't be able to tempt you because of your lack of self-control."*

Husbands and wives are supposed to have regular sex. It is how marriage was designed. Read through the Song of Solomon. Its description of the man and woman's intimate relationship reads like a kinky romance novel.

That is how our sexual relationships are supposed to work! Sex is not a bad thing. It is a great thing designed for marriage. It is our decadent culture that has turned it into sinful behavior.

Regular sex with your spouse will give you physical release and will also help heal damage done by your sexual addiction. In addition, the less you look at porn, the more attractive you will find your spouse.

For single men who are not married, double down on the other physical ways to release tension I mentioned above. Masturbation without porn is not a solution. There are varying schools of thought as to whether masturbation itself is a sin, but I do not believe it is a viable alternative to sex or porn. It still requires lustful thought and will inevitably lead to looking at porn. Instead, work on finding healthy ways to release tension like the ones we have discussed in this chapter. Find alternative ways to release anxiety, reduce stress, and avoid temptation.

To live porn free, you must stay physically active and find healthy ways to release tension.

QUESTIONS TO CONSIDER

1. Are you physically active? What do you do for exercise? Do you need to join a gym or start working out?

_____

_____

_____

_____

2. How can a lack of physical activity lead you towards porn and relapse?

_____

_____

_____

_____

3. What are some ways you can seek adventure in your life? What can you do to keep things exciting?

_____

_____

_____

_____

4. How often do you and your spouse have sex? (if applicable)

_____

_____

_____

_____

5. What are some healthy ways you can release stress and anxiety?

_____

_____

_____

_____

EXCERCISE EXCERCISE

This exercise is about, well, exercise. Create a weekly workout and exercise routine to keep yourself in shape, reduce stress, and release tension. You should be doing some sort of physical activity every day. I recommend resting on Sundays and spending the day with your family and in worship.

Monday

_____

_____

_____

Tuesday

_____

_____

_____

Wednesday

_____

_____

_____

Thursday

_____

_____

_____

Friday

_____

_____

_____

Saturday

_____

_____

_____

TIMOTHY REIGLE

9
ESTABLISH ROUTINE

Establishing a routine is vital to living porn free. Routines help you stay consistent in your battle. They encourage good habits and help you to avoid situations where you might be vulnerable to temptation.

Routines allow you to achieve small victories; building momentum to work towards accomplishing larger goals.

Beginning your day with a routine not only establishes good habits to start your day, but it also achieves small accomplishments that you can build on throughout the day. So even if your day gets shot to hell by lunch, you have at a minimum accomplished these small tasks.

In the same way, ending your day with an evening routine provides a proper close to your day and prepares you for bed.

For many men, including myself, evenings were when I was most vulnerable to temptation. I would often stay up late watching T.V., scrolling social media, or working on the computer. I would inevitably be triggered by some sort of sexual image, or simply from boredom.

Establishing routine took away those opportunities for relapse. I put together a routine that enabled me to avoid those temptations, while at the same time providing ways to decompress, alleviate stress, prepare for bed, and spend time with God.

Routines are different for each person, but these are five aspects that I believe make up an effective routine.

1. TURN OFF THE DEVICES

One of the biggest aspects of my routine was avoiding all electronic devices after a certain time each night. For myself and many other men, our addiction lived on our devices. I would be scrolling through my phone late at night, an image would trigger me, then before I knew it, I was on a porn site or messaging someone I should not have been messaging. Turning off the phone, computer, and TV will take away any opportunity to look at porn. Avoiding all that blue light late at night will also help you sleep better.

2. SOLITUDE

Find time each day to spend a few minutes alone in a quiet place. We need this time to relax, clear our minds, and process our thoughts. I know I was always much more likely to act on my sexual addiction when I was overwhelmed and felt like my brain was going to explode.

A perfect example to follow is Jesus. The Bible recounts many times where Jesus "went away by himself". Even the Son of God needed time away from the disciples and the crowds to clear His mind and pray.

Use this time to read Scripture, Pray, and Meditate. Read a short chapter of the Bible each day to stay grounded in the Word and find hope and encouragement. Spend time with God in prayer. Open your heart to Him. Lay down your burdens. Ask Him for help and guidance. I have heard it said that prayer is when you speak to God; meditation is when God speaks to you. Spend time in still silence and meditation. Breathing exercises are a great way to calm your mind, clear distractions, and focus. We all need to, as Psalm 46 says, "Be still and know that I am God."

In our routine, we should take the time to find solitude in a quiet place.

3. JOURNALING

Any good routine should include journaling. We already discussed the importance of journaling in Chapter 7. This is a great time to incorporate your daily journaling exercises.

4. READ BOOKS

I believe the most underrated and under-appreciated way to improve your life is through books.

However, far too many men do not read at all. They say they do not have time, or they do not have the attention span, or books are too expensive. Yet they binge watch Netflix, stay glued to a sports game for three hours, and spend tons of money on cable or streaming services. They choose the instant gratification of digital media over the time-tested method of learning from books.

In your journey to living porn free, reading books is a great way to educate yourself, focus your mind, and improve your life.

There is a plethora of books on pornography and sex addiction. I strongly recommend reading a few to further understand your addiction and to find tools to help you fight back.

Some of the books I have read on sex addiction were life-changing for me. They helped me understand the medical and physical side of compulsion and addiction. They encouraged me to have a close relationship with God in order to find healing and redemption.

Books are also a much better way to spend time than mindlessly scrolling through your phone and potentially being tempted to act out.

Here is a list of books I strongly recommend. Some are focused on sex and porn addiction. Others are religious or focus on masculinity.

Going Deeper – Eddie Capparucci

Surfing For God – Michael John Cusick

Wired For Intimacy – William M. Struthers

Every Man's Battle – Stephen Arterburn

Your Brain On Porn – Gary Wilson

Worthy of Her Trust – Jason Martinkus

Wild At Heart - John Eldredge

Jesus Is Better Than Porn – Hugh Houston

Disciplines of a Godly Man – R. Kent Hughes

Pilgrim's Progress – John Bunyan

A Purpose Driven Life – Rick Warren

There are many, many great books beyond this list. But these are all books I have read and have had a great impact on my life and my journey. I strongly recommend each one.

TIMOTHY REIGLE

5. SLEEP

Sleep is hugely underestimated by most men. Sleep is critical for stress control, weight management, mood regulation and even addiction recovery.

If you are sleep deprived, you will not have the strength to resist temptation. You will be much more stressed which will inevitably lead to the need to "escape". You will feel lethargic and will lack the motivation to stay sober.

As part of your routine, make sure you are getting 7-8 hours of sleep each night. Also, establish a consistent bedtime and wake up time. You will not achieve quality, regular sleep if your bedtime varies four hours every night.

Make sure you are getting good *quality* sleep as well. It will improve your stress levels, fight off depression, and allow you to start each day from a place of strength.

Combine these five steps into a routine and make it part of your daily life.

Routines build strong habits and establish consistent achievements. Build on these small victories throughout your day to tackle larger tasks. Then you are able to end the day on a positive note, clearing your mind and preparing for rest.

Routines establish consistency which leads to results.

In your battle to live porn free, it is essential that you establish routine.

QUESTIONS TO CONSIDER

1. What are some ways that establishing a routine could help you avoid relapse?

_____

_____

_____

_____

_____

2. Would avoiding electronic devices help you to avoid temptation?

_____

_____

_____

_____

3. Why is spending time in solitude important?

_____

_____

_____

_____

TIMOTHY REIGLE

4. Make a list of five books you want to read in the next couple of months.

_____

_____

_____

_____

_____

5. What are some ways you can make sure you get more and better sleep?

_____

_____

_____

_____

ESTABLISHING ROUTINE EXCERCISE

List five things you can do each morning as a helpful routine

1. _____

2. _____

3. _____

4. _____

5. _____

List five things you can do each evening as a helpful routine

1. _____

2. _____

3. _____

4. _____

5. _____

Here are some regular activities that you can add to your routine to help you in your plan to defeat porn addiction.

Daily: Prayer, Scripture, Journaling, Meditation, Reading A Book.
Weekly: Counseling/Therapy/Coaching, Support Groups, Exercise 3-4 Times, Rest and Refreshment, Church and Christian Fellowship, Check In With Support System.

TIMOTHY REIGLE

10
NEVER GIVE UP

I have referred to pornography and sex addiction as a "battle" multiple times throughout this book.

That is because it *is* a battle. It is a war with yourself, with your mind, with sin, and against the enemy who is trying to bring you down.

In battle, there are ups and downs, ebbs and flows, give and take. Some days are victorious. Other days you get beaten down and are forced to retreat.

It is ok to be in a struggle. Struggling with porn addiction is good. A struggle means there is a force trying to win against another force. If there was not a struggle, you would not be fighting back. You would have already been defeated.

But you ARE fighting back. Just by reading this book you are taking action to win this battle.

The Apostle Paul, in his letter to the Romans, chapter 7, discusses his own struggle with sin.

> *"I don't really understand myself, for I want to do what is right, but I don't do it. Instead, I do what I hate. But if I know that what I am doing is wrong, this shows that I agree that the law is good. So, I am not the one doing wrong; it is sin living in me that does it.*
>
> *There is another power within me that is at war with my mind. This power makes me a slave to the sin that is still within me. Oh, what a miserable person I am! Who will free me from this life that is dominated by sin and death? Thank God! The answer is in Jesus Christ our Lord."*

Like Paul, we know that our addiction is sinful. We know it is wrong and we have to find a way to stop. But even when we want to do what is right, we still end up failing. We do not want to keep looking at porn, but we keep doing it anyway.

It is the power of sin that lives inside us that we must overcome. We overcome through the grace and forgiveness of Jesus Christ. He will never give up on us. So, we must never give up ourselves.

Keep on fighting. Keep trying. Do not lose hope. Stay in the fight even when it seems like you are losing. There will still be days that you fail. There will still be occasions where you succumb to temptation and look at porn.

It's OK.

This journey is a marathon. We are in this for the long haul. You will not read this book and instantly be healed from addiction. You WILL slip up again. You WILL relapse. We all do.

The key is to never, ever give up.

Do not let a slip up ruin all your progress. Remember, two steps forward, one step backward is still moving forward.

If you do fail, admit it to yourself, to your support system, and to God. Then get right back on the wagon and start fresh from there.

Take this journey one day at a time. Maybe even an hour or a minute at time. If it is a tough day, just try to make it through that day.

Do not worry about going a week without porn before you have gone a day without porn. You cannot win this battle all at once. It will not happen. Keeping fighting day after day, week after week, month after month.

Consistently winning the small battles is the only way to win the larger war. You have not lost the battle unless you surrender. Keep fighting. Build on the small victories. Once you get a day, get another. Once you make it through a week, get another. Then a month. Then a year.

Remember, if you need help and guidance, I offer one-on-one coaching to assist you in your battle with sexual addiction. Please do not hesitate to reach out to me for help at timothy@intothewildernessblog.com or DM on Twitter @TimothyReigle.

Keep fighting. You know you can do it. You have what it takes to win deep inside you.

When you do not feel strong enough, trust in God. He will give you the strength.

I will be pulling for you brother. I believe in you. If I can overcome this addiction, anyone can. I will be praying for you. You can do it.

One day at a time. One battle at a time. One victory at a time.

Never give up.

QUESTIONS TO CONSIDER

1. Why is porn addiction referred to as a "battle"?

_____

_____

_____

_____

2. Can you relate with the Apostle Paul's struggle with sin?

_____

_____

_____

_____

3. Explain how the sin that lives inside us causes us to fail even when we know what the right thing is to do.

_____

_____

_____

_____

TIMOTHY REIGLE

4. What should you do if you relapse?

_____

_____

_____

_____

5. What are some things you can do to make sure you never give up?

_____

_____

_____

_____

BUILD YOUR BATTLE PLAN EXERCISE

As you continue on your journey to living porn free, you are going to need a battle plan. Use this exercise to set short-term and long-term goals and describe the tools and methods you will use to achieve them.

Short Term Goals (3-6 months)
These are goals you can expect to accomplish in a relatively short period of time. Keep these goals simple. The point is to build momentum through small measurable victories. Examples: Reduce porn relapses by 50%, Discover emotional wounds, Find local group to connect with.

_____

_____

_____

_____

Long Term Goals (6 months – 1 year+)
These are your ultimate goals. This is where you see yourself being when you have finally defeated porn. Examples: Porn and masturbation free, Strong friends and support system, Healthy and honest marriage.

_____

_____

_____

_____

How Will I Get There?

These are the steps you will take and the methods you will use to accomplish your goals.
Examples: Meet bi-weekly with a coach, Establish daily routines, Install accountability software on devices.

_____

_____

_____

_____

_____

_____

TIMOTHY REIGLE

CONCLUSION

My prayer for you at the beginning of this book was that you had reached the point in your life where you decided enough was enough and it was time to take control of your life.

You finally got to the point where you could no longer continue doing the same things over and over again and expect a different result.

You picked up this book because you wanted to live porn free. You went through each step and implemented the changes you need to make. You used the tools I recommended to fight back against your addiction.

Now you are beginning to turn the tide of the war. You have been able to go multiple days, maybe even weeks or months without looking at porn.

Your mind is clearer, your thoughts are pure, your relationship with your wife is improving. You are finding healing through the love and redemption of Christ.

Continue to use the tools I have laid out in this book to win the battle:
- × Admit there is a problem.
- × Seek God's help.
- × Find your Nathan.
- × Join a support group.
- × Discover why you are addicted.
- × Remove triggers.
- × Journal your progress.
- × Find ways to release tension.
- × Establish routine.
- × Never give up.

You can do it brother. You can win this battle.

You can live porn free.

God Bless.

TIMOTHY REIGLE

COACHING

If after reading this book you still feel overwhelmed by your addiction and need further help, I offer one-on-one coaching. I can come alongside and personally support you in your battle. I will provide guidance to create a plan to fight your addiction and accountability to keep you on track. We will work together to find the root cause of the problem and create ways to avoid triggers and relapse. I have already helped dozens of men battle their addictions; all who thought they were helpless. I'd love for you to be the next man to find freedom.

Contact me at timothy@intothewildernessblog.com or Direct Message me on Twitter @TimothyReigle if one-on-one coaching could help in your battle to live porn free.

ADDITIONAL RESOURCES

For more content visit my blog
www.intothewildernessblog.com

EMAIL SIGNUP

Sign up for my email list to get regular messages on porn addiction, faith, and masculinity delivered right to your inbox!

https://intothewildernessblog.com/email-signup/

FOLLOW ME ON TWITTER

https://twitter.com/TimothyReigle

ABOUT THE AUTHOR

Timothy Reigle is the founder of *Into The Wilderness*, a ministry dedicated to helping men transform their lives by renewing their faith, re-energizing their families, and restoring their masculinity. He is a licensed Chaplain and works with men through Bible study, preaching, and coaching to overcome pornography addiction and become better men. He lives in Pennsylvania with his wife and two daughters.

Made in the USA
Coppell, TX
09 September 2021